THROUGH THE AMERICAN WEST

by VALERIE BODDEN

CREATIVE EDUCATION

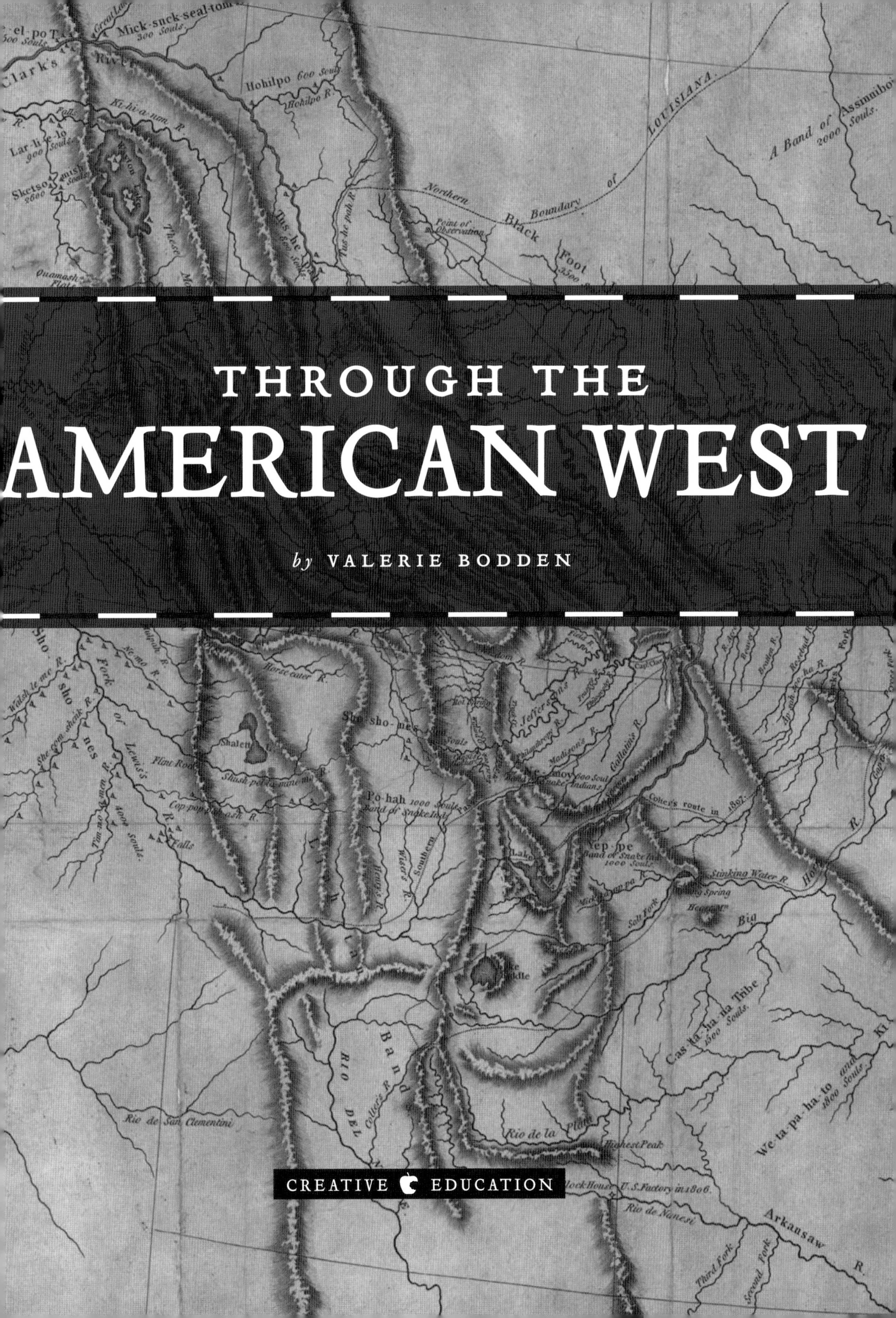

PUBLISHED BY Creative Education
P.O. Box 227, Mankato, Minnesota 56002
Creative Education is an imprint of The Creative Company
www.thecreativecompany.us

DESIGN AND PRODUCTION BY Ellen Huber
ART DIRECTION BY Rita Marshall
PRINTED BY Corporate Graphics
in the United States of America

PHOTOGRAPHS BY
Alamy (Mary Evans Picture Library, North Wind Picture Archives),
Corbis (Bettmann, Blue Lantern Studio), Getty Images (Apic, David David Gallery,
De Agostini Picture Library, Edward Hicks, Fotosearch, Mansell/Time & Life Pictures,
MPI, Stock Montage, SuperStock), The Granger Collection, NYC, History-map.com,
iStockphoto (Mike Bentley, Brandon Laufenberg), Jim Rowan Photography

LIBRARY OF CONGRESS CATALOGING-IN-PUBLICATION DATA
Bodden, Valerie.
Through the American West / by Valerie Bodden.
p. cm. — (Great expeditions)
Includes bibliographical references and index.
Summary: A history of Meriwether Lewis and William Clark's famed 1804–06 journey, detailing the challenges encountered, the individuals involved, the discoveries made, and how the expedition left its mark upon the world.

ISBN 978-1-60818-065-3
1. Lewis and Clark Expedition (1804–1806)—Juvenile literature. 2. Lewis, Meriwether, 1774–1809—Juvenile literature. 3. Clark, William, 1770–1838—Juvenile literature. 4. West (U.S.)—Discovery and exploration—Juvenile literature. I. Title.

F592.7.B64 2011
917.804'2—dc22 2010033413
CPSIA: 110310 PO1383

First Edition
2 4 6 8 9 7 5 3 1

Table of Contents

Westward Expansion

As the 19th century dawned, the United States was a new but growing country. Its borders extended from the Atlantic Ocean in the east to the Mississippi River in the west. Beyond that, the land was a mystery—until Meriwether Lewis and William Clark led a band of explorers known as the Corps of Discovery west and reached the Pacific Ocean in 1805. Reports of what they discovered—fertile land, rugged mountains, furbearing animals, and native peoples—would help to shape the very boundaries of the nation, which stretched from sea to sea by the middle of the century.

American settlers who moved west during the 1800s usually traveled in covered wagons, which were sometimes called "prairie schooners."

When the Corps of Discovery set out for their first winter camp in 1803, the population of the U.S. was 5.3 million, and two-thirds lived within 50 miles (80.5 km) of the Atlantic coast. Yet ever since settlers had begun arriving in North America in the 16th century, there had been people who had pushed the FRONTIER farther west. Although the Appalachian Mountains created a formidable natural barrier to expansion, rumors of rich land and abundant wild game on the western side of the range enticed many pioneers to make the westward trek. Between 1764 and 1774, the frontier moved nearly 17 miles (27 km) farther west each year.

After the U.S. won its independence from Great Britain in 1783, the westward trickle of settlers surged. Travelers clogged the four rough roads that spanned the Appalachians, and flatboats carrying settlers and their belongings crowded the Ohio River. By 1800, two new states—Kentucky and Tennessee—had been formed west of the Appalachians, with a combined population of more than 300,000. As people continued to settle in

As far back as the 1600s, Europeans who wanted to claim land in America had made treaties with the natives living in that place.

the area, many of the adventurers who had first crossed the mountains picked up and moved farther west. The frontier continued to advance in this manner until it reached the eastern banks of the Mississippi River.

Life on the frontier was hard. Homes and farms tended to be isolated, and families had to provide everything, including medical care, for themselves. Natural disasters such as floods or droughts could ruin an entire year's crop, and wild animals often killed livestock. In addition, frontier families faced a nearly constant threat from the American Indians on whose lands they had settled. Despite the fact that the U.S. government tried to establish TREATIES and buy lands from the Indians before settlers arrived, those agreements were not always accepted by the Indians nor honored by the government. As Americans grew hungrier for more land, the Indians were pushed farther and farther west. Sometimes

EXPEDITION JOURNAL

SERGEANT JOHN ORDWAY
letter to his parents, April 8, 1804

I am well thank God, and in high Spirits. I am now on an expidition to the westward, with Capt. Lewis and Capt. Clark, who are appointed by the President of the united States to go on an expidition through the interior parts of North America. We are to ascend the Missouri River with a boat as far as it is navigable and then to go by land, to the western ocean, if nothing prevents, &c.... We are to Start in ten days up the Missouri River.... We expect to be gone 18 months or two years.

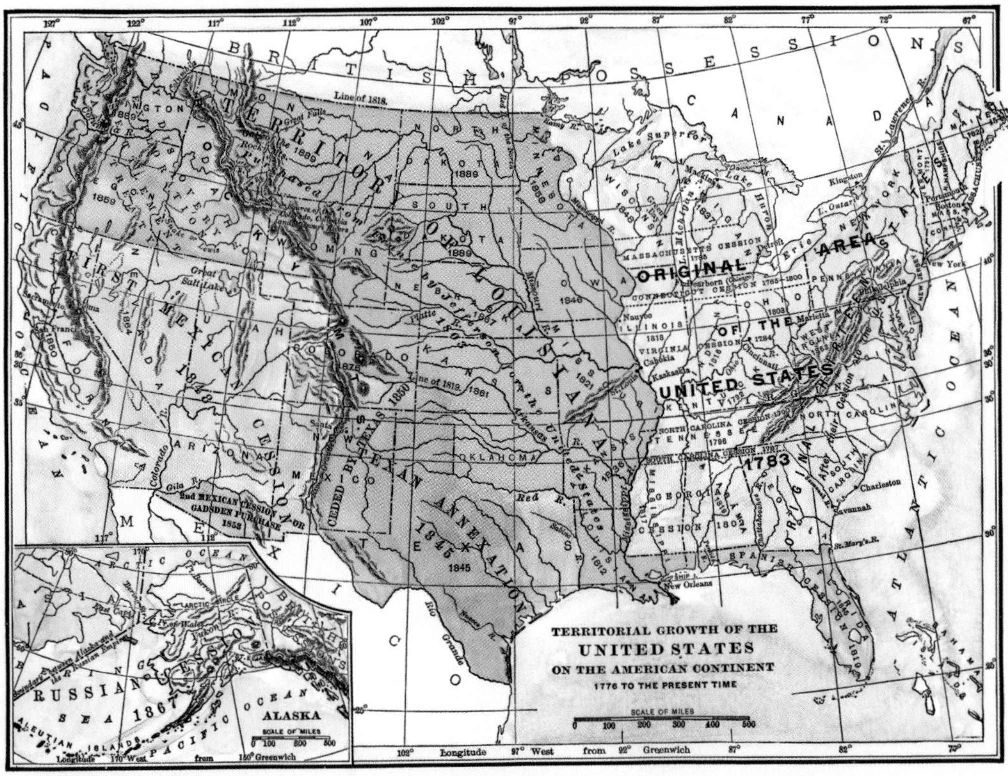

they pushed back against the white settlers, attacking individual homes and farms and even entire villages, leading to Indian wars that were devastating to both sides.

The U.S.'s territory greatly expanded throughout the 1800s (above), and its holdings eventually stretched to the Pacific Northwest's Columbia River (opposite).

As the nation's population continued to move westward, some people began to wonder about the possibilities that lay on the other side of the Mississippi River. That land was not owned by the U.S., however. During the early 1800s, France ruled Louisiana, a vast tract of land that stretched from the Mississippi in the east to the Rocky Mountains in the west, and from the Gulf of Mexico in the south to the Canadian border in the north. And France was not the only competitor on the continent. Spain controlled much of the western territory, from the Gulf of Mexico to the Pacific Ocean (and had ruled Louisiana from

1762 to 1800), Britain owned Canada, and Russia had entered Alaska. In the Pacific Northwest, Britain, Spain, Russia, and the U.S. all laid claim to the Oregon Country (present-day Idaho, Washington, and Oregon, along with parts of Montana and Wyoming).

One person who was most eager to learn more about the western reaches of the continent was Thomas Jefferson, who became the nation's third president in 1801. Jefferson's curiosity about the West was legendary, and by the time he entered the White House, his home library held more books about the American West than any other library in the world. Because white men had traveled only as far as the Great Bend of the Missouri River (near present-day Bismarck, North Dakota), most of the books relied on hearsay and outright speculation. Maps could pinpoint only three locations: the Great Bend, the city of St. Louis, and the mouth of the Columbia River (on the border between present-day Oregon and Washington), which American captain Robert Gray had discovered in 1792. Beyond that, some mapmakers thought that the Rocky Mountains were narrow and gentle and that California was an island. As far as the land was concerned, some authors thought that it held mountains of pure salt and was inhabited by woolly mammoths, Peruvian llamas, seven-foot-tall (2.1 m) beavers, and thin, friendly bison.

Jefferson and others who dreamed about the West believed that it contained a Northwest Passage, an all-water route across North America connecting the Atlantic and Pacific oceans. Since the time of Christopher Columbus, countries had yearned to find and control such a passage, which would allow for easier trading of goods—especially valuable American furs—with Asia. An all-water route

Corps of Discovery Profile: Sacagawea

In 1800, when she was about 12 years old, Sacagawea, a Shoshone Indian, was taken captive by a Hidatsa war party. Afterward, a French-Canadian trader named Toussaint Charbonneau either bought or won her and made her his wife, and they lived among the Hidatsa Indians. Although Sacagawea was only 16 or 17 years old when she joined the Corps of Discovery, Lewis wrote that she was as brave as anyone on the expedition. For most of the journey, Sacagawea carried her infant son, Jean Baptiste, on her back. During the return journey, Sacagawea and her family left the Corps at the Hidatsa villages. When Jean Baptiste was six, his parents brought him to Clark to be raised in St. Louis. In 1812, Sacagawea gave birth to a daughter but died a few months later.

would allow ships to cut through the continent instead of making the long, dangerous journey around the Cape of Good Hope in Africa or Cape Horn in South America. Jefferson also believed that finding a route across the continent to the Oregon Country would give weight to America's claims to that area and make it possible for the U.S. to one day rule the entire continent, from the Atlantic to the Pacific.

The high peaks of the Rocky Mountains posed a challenge to many explorers, including Sir Alexander Mackenzie, who traveled mainly by boat.

In 1793, a desire to discover the Northwest Passage had led Scottish-Canadian fur trader Sir Alexander Mackenzie to set off across the Canadian wilderness. Although he successfully crossed the Rocky Mountains and reached the Pacific coast, the trail he took was too difficult to be of use in establishing trade routes. Still, the 1801 published account of Mackenzie's journey, in which he encouraged the British government to set up a land-based trading route across western Canada to the Pacific Ocean, caught Jefferson's attention. The American president realized that such a step would give Britain control of not only the lucrative North American fur trade but the Oregon Country as well. Unwilling to let that happen, Jefferson decided that the U.S. needed to send its own expedition across the continent to solidify American claims to the West. To lead this effort, he called on his personal secretary, Meriwether Lewis.

Assembling the Corps

BORN IN 1774 IN VIRGINIA, ONLY MILES FROM JEFFERSON'S HOME AT MONTICELLO, MERIWETHER LEWIS HAD BEEN ACQUAINTED WITH THE FAMOUS STATESMAN SINCE HIS CHILDHOOD. AT THE AGE OF 18, LEWIS HAD ASKED JEFFERSON TO MAKE HIM LEADER OF A PLANNED (BUT NEVER COMPLETED) EXPEDITION TO THE WEST, BUT JEFFERSON THOUGHT HE was too young. The adventure-seeking man was never far from Jefferson's thoughts, however, and when Jefferson became president in 1801, he asked 27-year-old Lewis, who was then serving as a PAYMASTER in the army, to become his secretary.

By the next year, Jefferson had asked Lewis to lead an expedition across the continent. Despite his limited formal education, Lewis had long been a student of the natural world, and he had a keen eye for detail. He was also a skilled outdoorsman, well practiced in horseback riding, hunting, and hiking. To bolster his existing skills, Lewis undertook an intense course of study. In the spring of 1803, he traveled to Philadelphia, Pennsylvania, to study BOTANY, zoology, astronomy, CARTOGRAPHY, and medicine under the leading scientists of the day.

Lewis and Clark left a legacy to future thrill-seekers, and the explorers have been depicted in such works as 1931's Boys' Book of Adventure.

As Lewis prepared for his cross-continental journey, he requested that a co-captain be added. He and Jefferson agreed on William Clark, a retired army captain under whom Lewis had served for a brief period several years earlier. Clark, who had spent much of his life in the frontier lands of Ohio and Kentucky, had even less formal education than Lewis, but his military career had given him valuable experience in fighting and negotiating with Indians, conducting land SURVEYS, and building wilderness forts. Clark

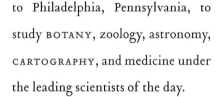

After studying law as a young man, Thomas Jefferson started his career in politics as a congressman, governor, and minister to France.

eagerly accepted Lewis's invitation.

Jefferson outlined his instructions for the explorers in a letter to Lewis, writing that the object of the expedition was to find "the most direct & practicable water communication across this continent"—in other words, they were to find the Northwest Passage. He instructed the leaders to take precise measurements of the positions of all river mouths, islands, and other landmarks to aid in map-making; to observe and describe all the plants and animals they encountered; and to study the soil and climate. They were also to learn everything they could about the Indian tribes of the West, making special note of their numbers, languages, customs, possessions, and politics.

On April 30, 1803, the expedition gained a new purpose with the U.S. purchase of Louisiana from France. For $15 million, the U.S. added 828,000 square miles (2.1 million sq km) to its area, doubling the size of the country. Now Lewis and Clark would be exploring American lands for most of their journey, and they were charged with spreading word of the land's new ownership to the Indians and traders they met along the way.

On July 5, 1803, Lewis left Washington, D.C., and headed for Pittsburgh, Pennsylvania, where he would pick up a specially made

EXPEDITION JOURNAL

Meriwether Lewis

April 7, 1805

Our vessels consisted of six small canoes, and two large perogues [sic]. This little fleet altho' not quite so rispectable as those of Columbus or Capt. Cook *were still viewed by us with as much pleasure as those deservedly famed adventurers ever beheld theirs; and I dare say with quite as much anxiety for their safety and preservation. we were now about to penetrate a country at least two thousand miles in width, on which the foot of civillized man had never trodden; ... and these little vessells contained every article by which we were to expect to subsist or defend ourselves.... I could but esteem this moment of my departure as among the most happy of my life. The party are in excellent health and sperits, zealously attached to the enterprise, and anxious to proceed; not a whisper of murmur or discontent to be heard among them, but all act in unison, and with the most perfect harmony.*

KEELBOAT and supplies before traveling down the Ohio River to meet Clark. The shallow keelboat was 55 feet (16.8 m) long and 8 feet (2.4 m) wide, with a covered cabin in the stern (back) and a covered hold in the bow (front). The boat was slow but strong, able to carry up to 12 tons (11 t) of cargo and withstand rough waters. Lewis loaded the boat with the rifles and ammunition on which the expedition would have to rely for both food and defense. He added numerous other supplies as well: paper and pencils for keeping journals, scientific instruments such as compasses and a telescope, hunting shirts (long, open-fronted shirts tied with a belt at the waist), hatchets, flints (for starting fires), mosquito netting, candles, tobacco, and whiskey. To treat illnesses, he packed powerful laxatives and emetics (to cause vomiting). He also included books on botany and navigation to serve as references during the journey. In addition, Lewis brought gifts for the Indians. Most were simple trinkets such as brass thimbles, combs, beads, buttons, and friendship medals.

The supplies bought for journaling were put to good use, as Lewis and Clark made note of many sights and experiences along the way.

With his keelboat loaded and ready, Lewis hired a handful of local soldiers and civilians to serve as his temporary crew and set off down the Ohio River toward Clark's home in Clarksville, Indiana Territory (in present-day southern Indiana), on August 31, 1803. The water level was low, and the going was slow and difficult, with the keelboat sometimes having to be pulled over sandbars. Along the way, Lewis added two canoes to his fleet, hoping to lighten the load of the larger keelboat. Finally, on October 14, he met up with Clark.

While waiting for Lewis to arrive, Clark had begun recruiting for

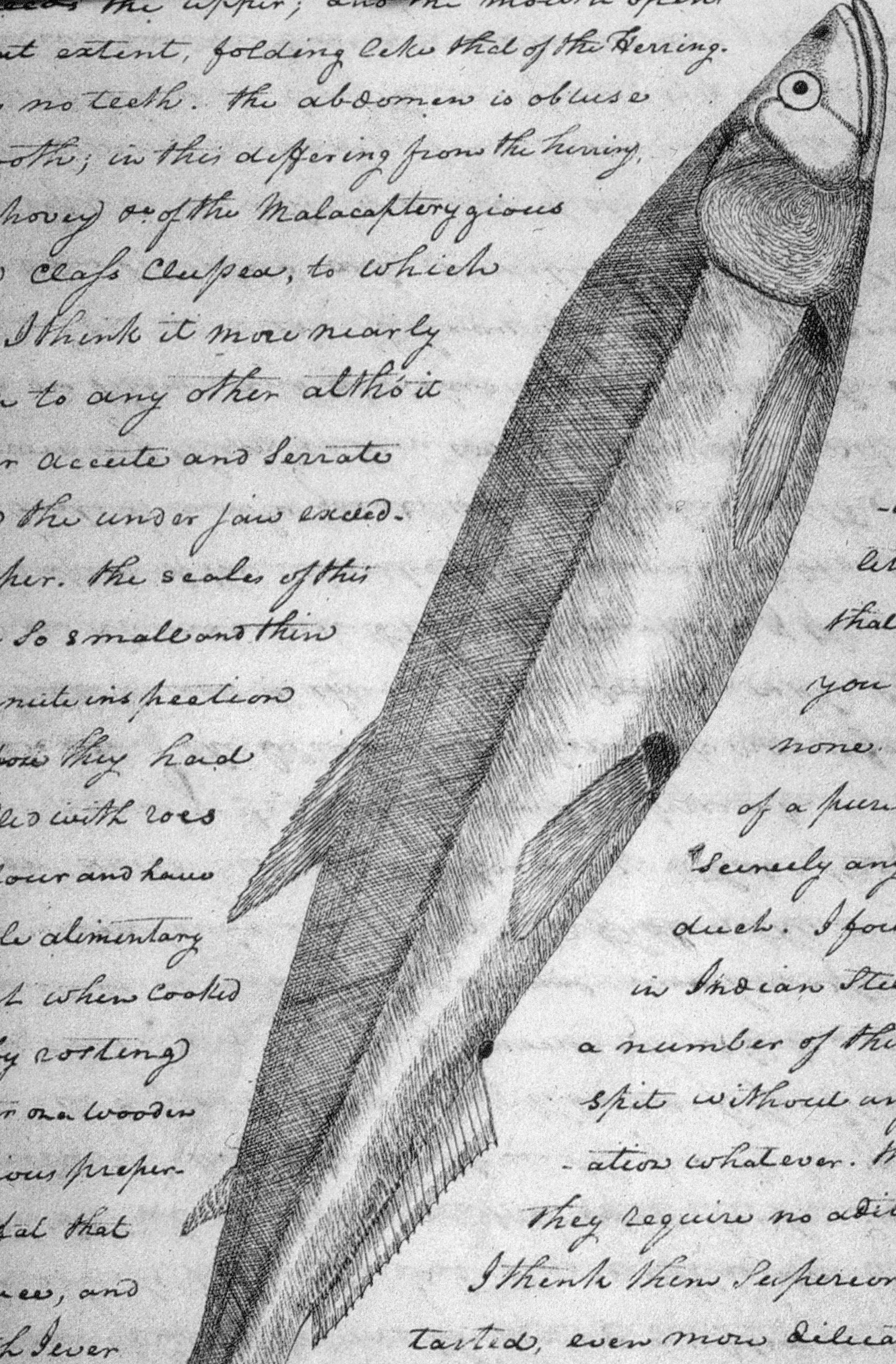

exceeds the upper; and the mouth opens to
great extent, folding like that of the Herring. it
has no teeth. the abdomen is obtuse and
smooth; in this differing from the herring, shad,
anchovey &c. of the Malacapterygious Order
and Class Clupea, to which howe-
-ver I think it more nearly allyed
than to any other altho' it has not
their accute and serrate abdomen
and the under jaw exceed- -ing the
upper. the scales of this little fish
are so small and thin that without
manute inspection you would
suppose they had none they are
filled with roes of a pure white
colour and have scarcely any percepti-
-able alimentary duct. I found them
best when cooked in Indian stile, which
is by roasting a number of them toge=
-ther on a wooden spit without any pre=
-vious prepar- -ation whatever. they are
so fat that they require no aditional
sauce, and I think them superior to any
fish I ever tasted, even more delicate and
lussious than the white fish of the Lakes
which have heretofore formed my standart
of excellence among the fishes. I have herd
the fresh anchovey much extalled but I hope I shall
be pardoned for believing this quit as good. the
bones are so soft and fine that they form no obstruction
in eating this fish.

the expedition. Although there was no shortage of volunteers, by the time Lewis arrived, Clark could recommend only seven men for the expedition, among them brothers Joseph and Reuben Field, Charles Floyd, and Nathaniel Pryor. Of the men who had accompanied Lewis down the Ohio, he invited two—George Shannon and John Colter—to remain with the expedition. These nine men were officially sworn into the army, as this was to be a military undertaking, and Floyd and Pryor were made sergeants. (A third sergeant, John Ordway, would later join the group.) The sergeants would manage the keelboat, keep their own journals, and issue commands to the other men, who were given the rank of private. Also joining the expedition was Clark's slave, York.

On October 26, Lewis, Clark, and their small "Corps of Discovery" began the journey from the Ohio to the Mississippi. Along the way, they met George Drouillard, the son of a French-Canadian father and Shawnee mother. Drouillard could speak French, English, and a couple of Indian languages, so he joined the expedition as an interpreter. On November 20, the Corps began to toil upstream against the Mississippi's mighty current, reaching Fort Kaskaskia, south of St. Louis, on November 28. There they took on more volunteers before continuing north past St. Louis to the mouth of the Wood River, where they established a winter camp. Throughout the winter, Lewis and Clark focused on obtaining additional supplies—including foods such as salted pork, flour, and corn, which brought their total food stores to seven tons (6.4 t). On May 14, 1804, with preparations complete, the Corps entered the mouth of the Missouri River, about to travel into a land previously only imagined by Americans in the East.

Corps of Discovery Profile: William Clark

William Clark was born on August 1, 1770, along the Rappahannock River in Virginia. When he was 14 years old, his family crossed the Allegheny Mountains and settled near Louisville, Kentucky. In 1789, Clark joined the Kentucky Militia and later transferred to the army, where he fought in a number of Indian wars. During the Corps of Discovery's westward journey, Clark drew nearly 200 maps, including a 4-foot-wide (1.2 m) map of the entire West. Although he relied on crude instruments and dead reckoning (estimating distance based on position and speed), his maps were amazingly accurate. After the expedition, Clark married and had five children. He served as superintendent of Indian Affairs and as governor of the Missouri Territory (1813–20) before his death on September 1, 1838.

Into the Unknown

From the moment they entered the Missouri, the members of the Corps of Discovery faced a battle against the mighty river. Toiling upstream, they had to navigate their keelboat and two pirogues (canoes made from hollowed-out tree trunks) around dangerous obstacles, including sandbars, whirlpools, and even whole trees hurtling downriver. When the winds were favorable, a sail could be raised on the keelboat, but more often than not, the men spent their days rowing, pulling the boats with ropes, or propelling them forward with long poles they dug into the river bottom. Each night, the Corps made camp along the river. Any animals the group's hunters had shot during the day were cooked; if there wasn't enough, pork and cornmeal or corn HOMINY and lard were distributed to each man. The hungry men each ate up to 9 pounds (4.1 kg) of meat per day.

The Missouri River presented many challenges to Lewis and Clark, not the least of which were the waterfalls that had to be bypassed.

Both on the river and in camp, the men waged a war against mosquitoes, which swarmed in their eyes, noses, ears, and mouths. They also faced strong thunderstorms, and with late summer came a nearly unbearable heat. The combination of insects and contaminated food also brought on physical ailments, such as pus-filled sores and diarrhea.

Despite such inconveniences, by mid-July, the Corps had traveled 600 miles (966 km) up the Missouri, and the land around them began to change dramatically, as thick forests were replaced by the tall grasses of the Great Plains. In early August, the members of the expedition met their first Plains Indians, members of the Oto and Missouri tribes, near the border of present-day Nebraska and Iowa. At a council with the tribes, the captains presented

Despite the language barriers—and with the help of interpreters—the explorers managed to communicate with all the Indians they met.

the Indian leaders with gifts and announced—as they would to all the tribes they encountered in U.S.-held territory—that the land they lived on was now ruled by a new "Great Father" in the East. The tribes welcomed the Americans and agreed to send a delegation to Washington, D.C., in the spring. During the council, Sergeant Charles Floyd became violently ill, and on August 20, he died of a ruptured appendix.

After burying Floyd, the expedition continued up the Missouri River into present-day South Dakota, where they met the friendly Yankton Sioux. By late September, however, they had entered the land of the more aggressive Teton Sioux, or Lakota. The Indians demanded that the Americans give them canoes, tobacco, or guns in return for safe passage up the river. When the captains refused, weapons were drawn, but a Teton chief eventually ordered his warriors to let the Americans pass, and violence was avoided.

As they followed the Missouri past Teton land, the men of the expedition marveled at the massive herds of bison, elk, and deer that

EXPEDITION JOURNAL

MERIWETHER LEWIS

August 12, 1805

The road took us to the most distant fountain of the waters of the mighty Missouri in surch of which we have spent so many toilsome days and wristless nights. thus far I had accomplished one of those great objects on which my mind has been unalterably fixed for many years, judge then of the pleasure I felt in allying my thirst with this pure and ice cold water which issues from the base of a low mountain or hill of a gentle ascent for 1/2 a mile.... after refreshing ourselves we proceeded on to the top of the dividing ridge from which I discovered immence ranges of high mountains still to the West of us with their tops partially covered with snow.

covered the plains. By now they had also begun to discover creatures not known in the eastern U.S., among which were coyotes, prairie dogs, and pronghorn. North of present-day Bismarck, North Dakota, the expedition was welcomed by the Mandan and Hidatsa Indians. In November, the Corps set up a winter fort near a Mandan village. The men remained there until April 7, 1805, when the keelboat—which was too big to navigate the upper reaches of the Missouri—was sent back downriver with a small contingent. The rest of the Corps climbed into their two pirogues and six small canoes to continue the journey west. Joining the group now were a French-Canadian fur trader named Toussaint Charbonneau and his 16- or 17-year-old Shoshone wife, Sacagawea (along with her 2-month-old baby), whom Lewis and Clark had asked to serve as interpreters.

Sacagawea was a valuable guide and a symbol of the expedition's peaceful intentions, as a woman would not have traveled with warriors.

In June 1805, the expedition made a grueling month-long, 18-mile (29 km) PORTAGE around the Great Falls of the Missouri, a stretch of river containing 5 massive waterfalls. By late July, the Corps had reached the eastern edge of the Rocky Mountains, and on August 12, Lewis and a small party found a mountain stream, which they believed to be the HEADWATERS of the Missouri River. Then the men continued up the mountain and over the CONTINENTAL DIVIDE. Expecting to find a great plain like the one they had just crossed, Lewis was stunned—and dismayed—to see tall, rugged, snow-covered mountains stretching endlessly into the distance.

The next day, Lewis met a party of Shoshone Indians led by Sacagawea's brother, Chief Cameahwait. The Shoshones greeted the expedition warmly, and by the end of August, the Indians had sold the Corps nearly 30 horses. A Shoshone guide named Old Toby agreed to lead the expedition over the Nez Percé Trail (now known as the Lolo Trail) through the Bitterroot Range of the Rocky Mountains.

Setting out on September 11, the Corps spent 11 days trekking up and down 160 miles (258 km) of steep mountainsides covered with thick undergrowth. Snow made the trail treacherous, and the horses sometimes slid down the steep slopes. Game was so scarce that the men had to kill some of their colts for meat, and eventually the only food sources remaining were bear's oil and candles.

Finally, the expedition emerged onto the Weippe Prairie in present-day Idaho. There the members rested in a village of friendly Nez Percé Indians and made the canoes that would carry them on the last leg of their westward journey. On October 7, 1805, the Corps slid its five new dugouts into the Clearwater River. The swift current carried the boats downstream to the Snake River and then on to the Columbia, which they entered on October 16. Leaving the forested mountains behind, the party entered the Great Columbian Plain, a dry land with few plants or animals.

One week after reaching the Columbia, the expedition members encountered a 55-mile-long (89 km) stretch of dangerous waterfalls and rapids, most of which they chose to run rather than portage. By the time they had exited this dangerous section of water, the men had passed into another new landscape, this one a lush, moist forestland. Huge Douglas firs, red cedars, and spruce towered above the river, and swans, geese, and sea otters were found in abundance. Best of all, the river widened and showed signs of being affected by a tide. The group rejoiced: they were almost at the Pacific.

Corps of Discovery Profile: Meriwether Lewis

Meriwether Lewis was born on August 18, 1774, on his family's plantation at Locust Hill, Virginia. As a young boy, he spent much of his time outdoors, learning from his mother about the plants that she used in herbal remedies. After some schooling, Lewis began to manage his family's plantation at the age of 18. In 1794, Lewis joined the army, and he was promoted to captain in 1800. The next year, he became president Thomas Jefferson's personal secretary. When he was asked to lead the Corps of Discovery, Lewis jumped at the chance, and he proved to be an able leader throughout the expedition. Afterward, however, Lewis fared poorly as governor of Upper Louisiana. He suffered from depression and began to drink heavily. On October 11, 1809, he committed suicide.

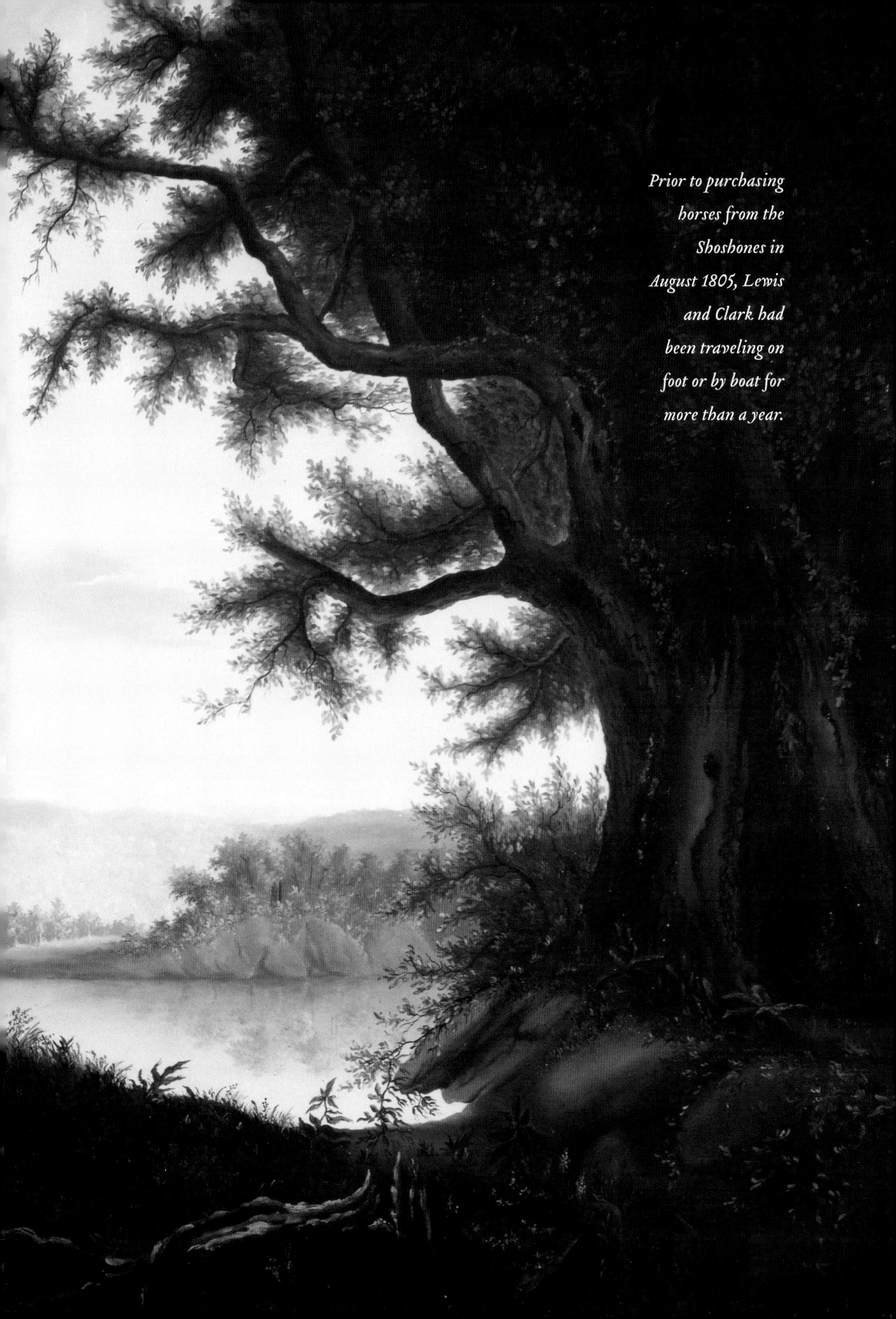

Prior to purchasing horses from the Shoshones in August 1805, Lewis and Clark had been traveling on foot or by boat for more than a year.

To the Ocean and Back

On November 7, 1805, Clark recorded an exuberant message in his field notes: "*Ocian in view*! O! the joy!" Unfortunately, his celebration was slightly premature, as what the Corps had spotted wasn't actually the Pacific but the estuary of the Columbia. The expedition tried to make its way closer to the coastline, but high waves, tides, and rain slowed progress for the next three weeks. Finally, several members of the party decided to make an overland trek to view the Pacific; they were amazed when they saw huge waves crashing against the cliffs below.

Of the hardy Chinooks encountered by the Corps on the Columbia River, Clark noted, "all go litely dressed ... in the coldest weather."

Since it was already late November, the Corps needed to quickly establish its winter quarters. Rather than choosing the location for the fort themselves, the captains turned the decision over to the members of the Corps for a vote. After everyone's vote was counted—including Sacagawea's and York's—the Corps decided to make camp on the south side of the Columbia River, near present-day Astoria, Oregon.

Though not cold, the winter proved to be rough for the members of the expedition, who had to survive almost entirely on lean elk meat that often became tainted in the mild climate. In addition, the nearly constant rain resulted in frequent illness and boredom. The Clatsop and Chinook Indians who lived nearby regularly visited the fort to trade goods for food, but the captains felt that the Indians demanded unreasonable prices, considering the Corps' low supply of wares. They were also annoyed by the Indians' thievery, as some natives helped themselves to the expedition's belongings.

By March, everyone was eager to leave Fort

Clatsop and head east. Before that could happen, the expedition needed new boats. The men traded with the nearby Indians for one canoe; then, unable to buy another, the captains authorized that one be stolen from a Clatsop village. Despite the fact that such theft was clearly against their own policies, the captains reasoned that the canoe made up for some elk that the Clatsop had stolen from them during the winter. On March 23, 1806, the Corps of Discovery set out for home. Although the men struggled to row against the Columbia's current, by the end of April, they had portaged the Columbia's falls and continued overland.

When Lewis and Clark heeded the advice of Indian guides, they found they could succeed in even the most treacherous situations.

In early May, the Corps arrived back at the Nez Percé village it had left seven months earlier. Since the Bitterroots were still covered with snow, the expedition remained among the Nez Percé for more than a month, but as mid-June approached, the captains grew impatient to cross the mountains and decided to set out. Only a day after entering the Bitterroots, however, they found themselves in snow more than 10 feet (3 m) deep, surrounded by raging creeks. Realizing that the conditions were too treacherous, the party made a dispirited return to the prairie. The Corps picked up several Indian guides before setting out across the mountains again on June 25. Thanks to the guides' skillful leadership, the party made it through the Bitterroots in only six days.

Now, instead of following the same route they had taken west, the captains decided to split the party to conduct further explorations of rivers that branched off the Missouri. Clark took a small group southward to survey the Yellowstone River, while Lewis's group

EXPEDITION JOURNAL

William Clark
September 16, 1805

Began to Snow [in the Bitterroots] about 3 hours before Day and Continud all day the Snow in The morning 4 Inches deep on The old Snow, and by night we found it from 6 to 8 Inches deep I walked in front to keep the road and found great dificuelty in keeping it as in maney places the Snow had entirely filled up the track.... a thickly timbered Countrey of 8 different kinds of pine, which are So covered with Snow, that in passing thro them we are continually covered with Snow, I have been wet and as cold in every part as I ever was in my life, indeed I was at one time fearfull my feet would freeze in the thin mockersons which I wore

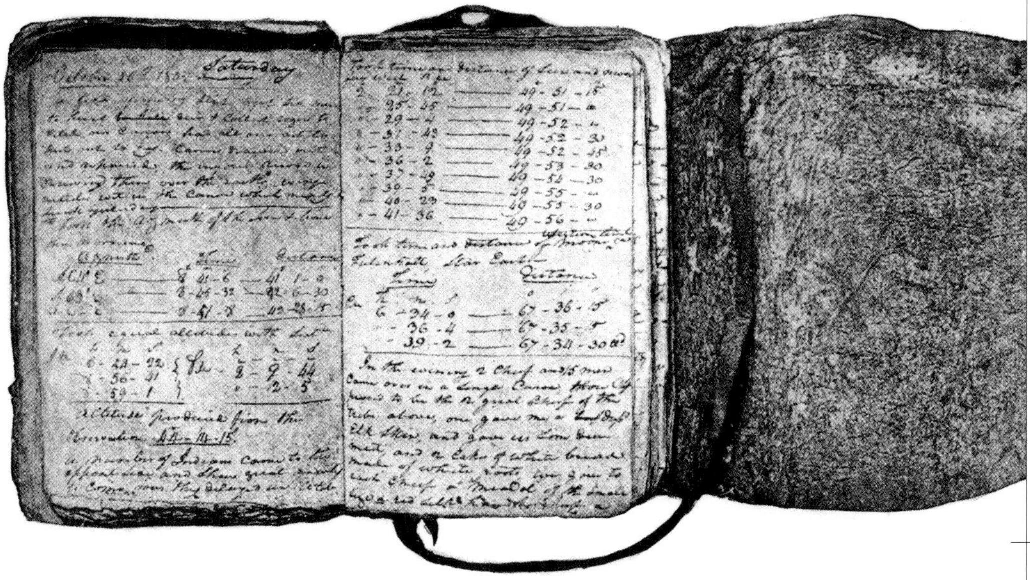

traveled north to explore the Marias River and determine the northernmost boundary of the Louisiana Purchase. When a small band of Blackfeet Indians stole several rifles and horses from Lewis's party, the white men killed two Indians and burned their camp.

Although reproductions of Clark's original journal are hard to come by, the full text may be found online and in many editions of books.

Afterward, Lewis and his men fled toward the Missouri River. When they arrived, Lewis decided that it was time to replenish the party's food supply. On August 11, he and Private Pierre Cruzatte were hunting for elk when Cruzatte accidentally shot Lewis in the buttocks. The day after the accident, Lewis's and Clark's parties were reunited, and they set off toward St. Louis together, with Lewis riding most of the way on his stomach because of the pain from his gunshot wound.

Finally, on September 23, 1806, 28 months and nearly 8,000 miles (12,875 km) after the expedition had begun, the Corps of Discovery returned to St. Louis. The men—who were believed to have died or gotten lost long before—were greeted by wild cheers and rifle salutes. After remaining in St. Louis for more than a month, Lewis and Clark set out for the East, where Lewis made his report to Jefferson in January 1807.

Large rodents in the same family order as rats, beavers are semi-aquatic animals that can remain underwater for as long as 15 minutes.

Ultimately, Lewis and Clark had completed their task of discovering "the most direct & practicable water communication across this continent." Unfortunately, as Lewis wrote to Jefferson, part of that route was through "tremendious mountains which for 60 [miles] are covered with eternal snows," a description that ended the dream of an American Northwest Passage. Still, the men's accounts of the land and its animals—especially furbearing ones such as beavers—led many Americans to follow in their footsteps. The Corps' exploration of the Pacific Northwest also helped to solidify U.S. claims there, and in 1846, American ownership

Corps of Discovery Profile: John Colter

John Colter was born near Staunton, Virginia, around the year 1774. At the age of five, he moved west with his family, settling in Maysville, Kentucky. After traveling with the Corps of Discovery to the Pacific and back to the Mandan villages in August 1806, Colter requested permission to return west as a fur trapper. The captains granted his request, and Colter became one of America's first MOUNTAIN MEN. During the winter of 1807–08, he became the first white man to discover the area that is today Yellowstone National Park. Soon afterward, he narrowly escaped being killed by a band of Blackfeet Indians by fleeing naked through the wilderness. Colter's later information about the Yellowstone and Wind River area was instrumental in helping Clark revise his 1814 map of the West.

HISTORY

OF

THE EXPEDITION

UNDER THE COMMAND OF

CAPTAINS LEWIS AND CLARK,

TO

THE SOURCES OF THE MISSOURI,

THENCE

ACROSS THE ROCKY MOUNTAINS

AND DOWN THE

RIVER COLUMBIA TO THE PACIFIC OCEAN.

PERFORMED DURING THE YEARS 1804—5—6.

By order of the

GOVERNMENT OF THE UNITED STATES.

PREPARED FOR THE PRESS

BY PAUL ALLEN, ESQUIRE.

IN TWO VOLUMES.

VOL. I.

of the Oregon Country south of the present-day Canadian border was recognized by Britain.

Despite Lewis and Clark's well-intentioned promises to the Indians that their new "Great Father" would make them prosperous through trade, many tribes soon found themselves being pushed off their land, and some were eventually forced to settle in Indian Territory in Oklahoma. Many who refused were slaughtered. Some of the men from the expedition, including George Drouillard, were themselves killed in attacks by Indians in later trading ventures. Other members of the Corps settled down to farm the 320 acres (130 ha) the government had awarded them at expedition's end. Both Lewis and Clark were appointed to government positions in the Territory of Upper Louisiana, Clark as superintendent of Indian affairs and Lewis as governor. While Clark excelled in his position, Lewis was too much of a businessman at heart to be at home in politics. He fell into a depression, and in 1809, he shot himself. Although the other members also died long ago, the adventures of the Corps of Discovery live on more than 200 years later in the million-plus words recorded in the men's journals—and in the continent-wide nation they helped to make possible.

Sadly, Lewis did not live to see even the first authorized publication (in 1814) of his and Clark's journals of their historic adventure.

TIMELINE

1770	William Clark is born along the Rappahannock River in Virginia on August 1.
1774	On August 18, Meriwether Lewis is born on a Virginia plantation near Thomas Jefferson's home, Monticello.
1783	The Revolutionary War ends, and the U.S. wins its independence from Great Britain.
1792	In May, American sea captain Robert Gray discovers the mouth of the Columbia River.
1792	Lewis seeks a place on a planned expedition to the West, but the 18-year-old is turned down.
1793	Scottish-Canadian fur trader Sir Alexander Mackenzie makes an overland crossing of Canada and arrives at the Pacific coast.
1800	At about the age of 12, Sacagawea is captured from the Shoshones by a Hidatsa war party.
1801	Thomas Jefferson is sworn in as president on March 4; Lewis is made his personal secretary.
1803	On February 28, Congress approves Jefferson's initial request of $2,500 for an expedition to the west.
1803	The treaty completing the Louisiana Purchase is signed on April 30 but is not announced until July.
1803	On August 31, Lewis begins the trip down the Ohio River to meet Clark at Clarksville, Indiana Territory.
1804	After wintering at Camp Wood, the Corps of Discovery begins its journey up the Missouri River on May 14.
1804	After Charles Floyd dies on August 20, the men vote for Patrick Gass to take his place as a sergeant.
1804	In October, the Corps arrives at the villages of the Mandan Indians in North Dakota and sets up winter quarters.
1805	On April 7, the Corps leaves its winter camp to continue up the Missouri River.
1805	Lewis crosses the Continental Divide on August 12.
1805	In September, the Corps spends 11 days crossing the Bitterroot Mountains.
1805	On November 7, the Corps enters the estuary of the Columbia.
1806	The Corps leaves its winter quarters near the Pacific to travel back east on March 23.
1806	On June 15, the Corps attempts to cross the Bitterroots but is forced to turn back.
1806	The Corps splits up on July 3 to complete a six-week exploration of the Marias and Yellowstone rivers.
1806	On September 23, the Corps of Discovery returns to St. Louis.

ENDNOTES

BOTANY: the study of plants

CAPTAIN COOK: James Cook, British naval officer and explorer who charted the coast of New Zealand and part of Australia in 1770 and led a search for a Northwest Passage north of Canada

CARTOGRAPHY: the skill or study of mapmaking

CONTINENTAL DIVIDE: a series of mountain ridges that runs from Alaska to Mexico and separates the rivers that flow east to the Atlantic from those that flow west to the Pacific

ESTUARY: the wide lower section of a river where it meets the sea, causing fresh and salt water to mingle, and is affected by the tide

FRONTIER: the farthest border of a settled area, usually inhabited by hunters, farmers, or other pioneers

HEADWATERS: the springs or streams that make up a river's source

HOMINY: food made from boiled, dried kernels of corn

KEELBOAT: a shallow, covered riverboat that can be rowed, pulled, or poled

MOUNTAIN MEN: men who lived alone in the mountains of western North America during the early 19th century, often as trappers

PAYMASTER: a person in charge of paying salaries

PORTAGE: an overland route across which boats and supplies must be carried to get from one waterway to another or to get past an unnavigable section of river

SURVEYS: measurements of a land area often taken for the purposes of making a detailed map

TREATIES: formal agreements between two or more countries or groups of people

SELECTED BIBLIOGRAPHY

Ambrose, Stephen. *Lewis & Clark: Voyage of Discovery*. Washington, D.C.: National Geographic Society, 1998.

——. *Undaunted Courage: Meriwether Lewis, Thomas Jefferson, and the Opening of the American West*. New York: Simon & Schuster, 1996.

Burns, Ken, and Dayton Duncan. *Lewis and Clark: The Journey of the Corps of Discovery*. DVD. Washington, D.C.: Florentine Films and WETA, 2004.

Jackson, Donald, ed. *Letters of the Lewis and Clark Expedition with Related Documents: 1783–1854*. Urbana: University of Illinois Press, 1962.

Lavender, David. *The Way to the Western Sea: Lewis and Clark across the Continent*. New York: Harper & Row, 1988.

Moulton, Gary, ed. *The Lewis and Clark Journals: An American Epic of Discovery*. Lincoln: University of Nebraska Press, 2003.

Public Broadcasting Service. "Lewis and Clark: The Journey of the Corps of Discovery." PBS Online. http://www.pbs.org/lewisandclark/index.html.

Smith, Page. *The Shaping of America: A People's History of the Young Republic*. New York: McGraw-Hill, 1980.

FOR FURTHER READING

Eisenberg, Jana. *Lewis and Clark: Path to the Pacific*. New York: Children's Press, 2005.

Fradin, Judith Bloom, and Dennis Brindell Fradin. *The Lewis and Clark Expedition*. New York: Marshall Cavendish Benchmark, 2008.

Gragg, Rod. *Lewis and Clark on the Trail of Discovery: The Journey That Shaped America*. Nashville, Tenn.: Rutledge Hill Press, 2003.

Isserman, Maurice, and John S. Bowman. *Across America: The Lewis and Clark Expedition*. New York: Chelsea House, 2010.

INDEX